Auge der Seherin - Stimme des Dichters

Eye of the Seeress - Voice of the Poet

ALSO BY RALPH METZNER

Allies for Awakening

The Toad and the Jaguar

Alchemical Musings

Birth of a Psychedelic Culture, with Ram Dass & Gary Bravo

The Ecology of Consciousness

Sacred Vine of Spirits – Ayahuasca (ed.)

Sacred Mushroom of Visions – Teonanácatl (ed.)

Green Psychology

The Unfolding Self

The Well of Remembrance

Through the Gateway of the Heart (ed.)

Know Your Type

Maps of Consciousness

The Ecstatic Adventure (ed.)

The Psychedelic Experience, with Timothy Leary & Richard Alpert

Auge der Seherin - Stimme des Dichters

Eye of the Seeress - Voice of the Poet

Völuspa / Edda   *Hildegard von Bingen*

Francesco d'Assisi   *Meister Eckhart*

Johann Wolfgang von Goethe   *William Blake*

Rainer Maria Rilke   *Bertholt Brecht*

Gesichte – Gedichte – Gebete
Visions – Poems – Prayers

Ausgewählt und übertragen
Selected and translated

Ralph Metzner

Four Trees Press

Graphics & Layout by Cynthia Smith

Printed in the U.S.A.

FOUR TREES PRESS
PO Box 692
El Verano, CA 95433
www.FourTreesPress.com

Prolog. 2

Edda / Völuspa (*circa* 800-1200). 4

Hildegard von Bingen (1099-1179). 40

Francesco d'Assisi (1181-1226). 46

Meister Eckhart (1260-1327) 50

Johann Wolfgang von Goethe (1749-1832) 56

William Blake (1757-1827). 62

Rainer Maria Rilke (1875-1926) 70

Bertholt Brecht (1898-1956). .74

Epilog I: Heracleitus 80
Epilog II: Talmud 82

Prolog

In diesem Buch habe ich mystische und visionäre Texte und Gedichte aus Tausend Jahren Europäischer Literatur gesammelt – Schriften, die mich besonders inspiriert und erfreut haben.

Ich wollte eine vollständig zweisprachige Sammlung zusammenstellen, weil Deutsch und Englisch die Sprachen meiner Kindheit und Jugend sind und ich die Literatur in beiden Sprachen liebe.

Ich habe Texte von Meister Eckhart, Goethe, Rilke und Brecht ins Englische übertragen und visionäre Gedichte von William Blake ins Deutsche.

Das *Lied von Bruder Sonne* des Franz von Assisi wurde ursprünglich auf Italienisch geschrieben. Ich habe Deutsche und Englische Übersetzungen als Grundlage meiner Versionen verwendet.

Die mystischen Gesichte und Gedichte der Äbtissin Hildegard von Bingen wurden zuerst aufgezeichnet auf Latein, der religiösen Schriftsprache ihrer Zeit, von ihrem Amanuensis, dem Mönch Volmar. Wir wissen nicht in welcher Sprache ihre Visionen zu ihr gesprochen haben. Auch hier habe ich existierende Übersetzungen als Ausgangspunkt meiner Versionen benützt. Ich habe in dem Buch *Das Mystische Grün* (Arun Verlag, 2000) über Hildegard's Lehre und Visionen von *Viriditas* geschrieben.

Der erste und längste Teil des Buches umfasst die *Völuspa*, einer der Gesänge aus der *Älteren Edda*. Dieses Lied stammt von einem unbekannten Autor in Island (möglicherweise einer Frau) in dem 10. Jahrhundert. Da dieses Lied in der Alt-Nordischen Sprache verfasst und geschrieben wurde, habe ich auch hier mehrere Deutsche und Englische Übersetzungen als Grundlage meiner Version verwendet. *Völuspa* bedeutet "Die Gesichte der Völva." Völvas waren Hellseherinnen, in der vorchristlichen nordischen Kultur. In diesem Gedicht erzählt eine ungenannte Völva ihre Visionen, als Antworten auf Fragen die ihr von Odin/Wodan, dem wahrheitsuchenden Gott der Schamanen und Dichter, gestellt werden.

Seit ich über die *Völuspa* in meinem Buch *Der Brunnen der Erinnerung* (Aurum Verlag, 1994) geschrieben habe, bewundere ich diese Dichtung – mit ihren erstaunlichen Visionen vom Ursprung der Welt, von den schöpferischen und kriegerischen Taten der Götter und Menschen, und den wuchtigen Prophezeihungen von planetarischer Zerstörung und Erneuerung, die in unserer Zeit scheinbar wahr werden.*

---

* Ich danke Manuel Aicher für seine sorgfältigen Korrekturen an meinen deutschen Versionen.

Prolog

In this book I have gathered mystical and visionary writings and poems from a thousand years of European literature – writings that have particularly inspired and delighted me.

I wanted to create a completely bilingual collection because German and English have been my native tongues from childhood and youth onward, and because I love the literature of both languages.

I translated German texts of Meister Eckhart, Goethe, Rilke and Brecht into English, and visionary poems of William Blake into German.

The *Canticle of Brother Sun* by Saint Francis of Assisi was originally written in Italian and I have consulted several English and German translations to arrive at my versions.

The mystical visions and poems of the Abbess Hildegard von Bingen were first recorded by her amanuensis, the monk Volmar, in Latin, the written religious language of her time. We do not know in what language her voices spoke to her. Here too, I have consulted existing English and German translations to arrive at my versions. I wrote about Hildegard's teachings and visions of mystical greenness *(viriditas)* in my book *Green Psychology* (Park Street Press, 1999).

The first and longest section of the book is taken up with the *Völuspa,* one of the songs of the *Elder Edda,* by an unknown author (perhaps a woman) around the 10th century, in Iceland. Since it was written in the Old Norse language and script, I have here too consulted several modern English and German translations to arrive at my versions. *Völuspa* means "Visions of the Völva." Völvas were clairvoyant seeresses in the pre-Christian Nordic culture. In this poem an unnamed völva is relating her visions in response to questions posed to her by Odin/Wodan, the knowledge-seeking god of shamans and poets.

Ever since I wrote about and quoted from the *Völuspa* in my book *The Well of Remembrance* (Shambhala, 1994), I have admired this poem with its awesome visions of the origins of the world, the creative activities and conflicts of gods and humans, and stunning prophecies of planetary destruction and renewal that seem to be coming true in our times.

Völuspa

Gesichte der Völva

Hört mich in Stille,
ihr heiligen Sippen,
ihr hohen und niederen,
Kinder des Heimdall.[1]

Du willst, Walvater[2],
dass wohl ich berichte
die älteste Kunde
der Welt, die ich weiss.

Ursprung der Welt

Ich weiss von den Riesen,
den erstgeborenen alten,
die mich in Urzeit
erzeugt und erzogen.

Weiss die neun Welten,
weiss auch neun Wurzeln
des herrlichen Baumes,
tief in der Erde.

Als nur Ymir[3] der Uralte,
der Riese auf Erde war,
gab's Sand nicht, noch See,
noch salzige Welle.

Die Erde nicht unten,
und oben kein Himmel,
nur gähnender Abgrund,
und auch wuchs kein Grass.Völuspa

---

[1] *Heimdall* ist der Torwächter unter den Asen, ähnlich wie der römische Janus; aber hier auch als Vater der Menschenrasse angesehen. Seine Gestalt ist weiss und leuchtend, und er besitzt ein Horn, das Gjallarhorn, dass man auf der ganzen Welt hören kann.

[2] *Walvater*, nord. *Valfödr*, "Vater der Gefallenen," ist einer von Odin's vielen Benennungen. Er bezieht sich auf die Vorstellung, das gefallene Krieger von Odin in Valhalla aufgenommen werden. (Man sagte dass gefallene Krieger, je nach Wahl auch zu Freyja gehen könnten.)

[3] *Ymir* ist der Name des Ur-Riesen, aus Flusswasser und Eis geformt, am Anfang der Erde. Aus seinen Armen und Füssen stammen die männlichen Bergriesen und weiblichen Flussriesen.

Völuspa

Visions of the Völva

Hear me in silence,
ye kin of the Holy Ones,
both the higher and lower,
the children of Heimdall[4].

You, Wodan[5], want me
to tell of the world,
as well as I know,
from the earliest times.

Origin of the World

I know of the giants,
primordial and great,
who raised me and fed me
in times long ago.

Nine worlds I know,
and nine great roots too,
of that wonderful tree,
so deep in the Earth.

There was only Ymir[6] the giant,
the Ancient on Earth,
there was no sand, no sea,
nor ocean waves.

No earth was there,
no heavens above,
only a gaping abyss,
and no grass growing.

---

[4] *Heimdall* is the name of celestial gate-keeper of the Aesir gods, akin to the Roman Janus; but here also regarded as progenitor of the human race. His form is white and luminous, and he has a horn, the Gjallarhorn, that can be heard around the world.

[5] Among the many epithets for Wodan or Odin, is the German *Walvater* – Father of the Fallen – pointing to his choosing of warriors killed in battle, who get chosen to go with him to Valhalla. (It was also said that fallen warriors could, if they wished, go to Freyja's domain after dying.)

[6] *Ymir* is the name of the primordial giant, formed from rivers and ice, in the beginnings of the Earth. From his arms and feet come male mountain giants and female river giants.

Des Riesen Burrs[7]
drei Göttersöhne,
erhoben den Boden.
So schufen sie Midgard[8],
die mächtige Welt.

Die Sonne von Süden,
schien auf den Steingrund;
da wuchs aus der Erde
das grünende Kraut.

Vom Süden die Sonne
die Schwester des Mondes,
schlang ihren Arm am
Rande des Himmels.[9]

Weder Sonne noch Sterne
wussten ihre Wohnung;
auch der Mond erkannte
noch nicht seine Macht.

Zum Richtstuhl gingen
die heiligen Götter;
die Berater begaben
sich also zum Rat.

Der Nacht und dem Neumond
gaben sie Namen;
auch Morgen und Mittag,
Zwielicht und Abend,
um zu messen die Zeit.

---

[7] *Burr*, auch *Borr*, heisst der Riese, der mit der Riesin *Bestla* die drei ersten Asengötter *Odin*, *Vili* und *Vé*, erzeugt hat. Das Geschlecht der Riesen war den Göttern auf der Erde vorausgegangen.

[8] *Midgard*, der "Garten der Mitte," ist die Biosphäre mit ihren Pflanzen, Tieren und Menschen.

[9] Diese und die nächste Strophe beschreiben Ereignisse aus der Vorgeschichte des Planeten—die Sonnenwendlaufbahn, "am Rande des Himmels," und die Entstehung des Mondes.

The three sons of Bor,[10]
both giants and gods,
they lifted the land, they
made mighty Midgard[11].

The sun from the South
shone bright on stoneground;
the sweet greening grass
grew then from the earth.

From the South came the Sun,
great sister of Moon,
extending her arm
along the edge of the sky.[12]

Neither sun nor the stars
were set in their places;
even Moon did not know
what power he had.

To gather in council
the Holy Ones came;
the councilors met
to converse and to speak.

Names they gave
to night and the Moon,
to morning and noontime as well;
to twilight and evening,
and the measures of time.

---

[10] *Bor*, or *Bur*, is the name of the giant who with the giantess *Bestla*, fathered the three first Aesir gods – *Odin*, *Villi* and *Vé*. The race of primordial giants preceded the gods on planet Earth.

[11] Midgard, the "garden in the middle," is the biosphere, with its plants, animals and humans.

[12] This verse and the next describe events from the pre-history of the planet—the course of the sun at the solstices, "along the edge of the sky," and the origin of the moon.

Asengötter, Riesen und Zwerge

Zum Felde von Ida[13]
kamen die Asen;
Altäre und Tempel,
bauten sie hoch.

Sie stellten die Schmiede
und hämmerten Erz:
sie schufen die Zangen,
der Werkzeuge viel.

Sie spielten am Brett,
ganz heiter im Hofe.
Nichts fehlte, auch nicht
das glänzende Gold.

Kamen mächtige Frauen,
drei Töchter der Riesen,
gewaltig und furchtbar,
aus Jötunheim[14] her.

Zum Richtstuhl gingen
die heiligen Götter;
die Berater begaben
sich wieder zum Rat:

Wer schaffen sollte
das Volk der Zwerge,
aus Brimirs Blut
und Bláinns Gebein?[15]

---

[13] Das *Ida-Feld* ist eine überirdische, "glänzende Ebene" wo die Götter sich befinden, vor der Schöpfung der Menschen und auch nach dem Ragnarök. Die Asen sind die Himmelsgötter, wie z.B. Odin und Thor.

[14] *Jötunheim* ist das Reich der Riesen – östlich und nordöstlich von Midgard, der Welt der Pflanzen, Tiere und Menschen.

[15] *Brimir* ist eine Umschreibung von Ymir, dem ursprünglichen Erdriesen, dessen Blut das Flusswasser ist, dessen Gebein die Steine. *Bláinn*, verwandt mit altnordisch *blar* – "blau," ist auch Ymir, dessen Schädel der blaue Himmel ist. Die Zwerge sind also die Geister der Berge und Flüsse, Gestein und Gewässer.

Aesir gods, giants and dwarves

On the great plains of Ida,
the Aesir[16] gods met;
shrines and great temples
they timbered on high.

They built the forges,
to hammer their ores;
made metal tongs,
and plenty of tools.

Boardgames they played,
content in their garden;
nothing was lacking,
even gold was there.

Then three mighty females
came, daughters of giants,
awesome and terrible,
from their giant-home.[17]

To gather in council
the Holy Ones came;
the councilors met, to
speak and to ask:

Who should create
the folk of the dwarves,
from Brimir's blood
and the bones of Bla'inn?[18]

---

[16] The *Ida-plains* are a supra-earthly domain, a "shining field" where the gods meet, before the creation of humans, and also at the end of the world, the ragnarök.

[17] *Jötunheim*, the realm of the giants, is situated to the East and Northeast of Midgard, the world of plants, animals and humans.

[18] *Brimir* is another name for Ymir, the primordial Earth-giant, whose blood are the rivers of Earth, whose bones are the stones. *Bla'inn*, related to the Old Norse *blár* – "blue," is another transliteration of Ymir, whose skull is the blue sky. Thus the dwarves are the spirits of mountains and rivers, stones and waters.

Motsognir[19] wurde der
mächtigste, unter
allen der Zwerge;
der Durin[20] der nächste.

Sie schufen viele
den Menschen ähnlich;
die Zwerge der Erde,
wie Durin es hiess.

Erschaffung der Menschen

Dann kamen drei
aus der Sippe der Asen[21],
mächtig und mild –
zum Meer kamen sie.

Sie fanden am Strand,
die Ask und die Embla,[22]
kraftlos und leblos-
kein Funke des Lebens.

Nicht Seele hatten sie,
auch keine Sinne,
weder Wärme des Lebens,
noch lichte Farben.

Odin gab ihnen Seele,
die Sinne der Hönir,
der Lodur die Lebenswärme
und lichte Farben.

---

[19] Der Zwergname *Motsognir* ist umstritten. Diese ersten Zwerge versuchten, Menschen zu gestalten. Frühzeitliche menschenähnliche Geschöpfe kommen in vielen eingeborenen Mythen vor.

[20] Ebenso der Name *Durinn*. Nach diesen beiden Strophen über die ersten Zwerge, folgt in the *Völuspá* eine ganze Reihe von Strophen mit Zwergnamen, die von diesen abstammen. Ich habe sie ausgelassen.

[21] Die drei Asen, die die Menschen erschaffen haben, sind *Odin, Hönir* und *Lodur*, die weiter unten erwähnt sind. In anderen Texten der *Edda* sind die drei schaffenden Asen *Odin, Vili* und *Vé*. Nur Odin spielt in dem weiteren Mythen und Schriften, auch der *Völuspá*, eine bedeutende Rolle.

[22] *Ask* bedeutet den Baum Esche, und *Embla* möglicherweise die Ulme. Das wäre also eine Erschaffung der Menschen aus Baumholz.

The one called Motsognir,[23]
of all of the dwarves,
was the mightiest by far;
and Durin[24] was next.

Many forms they created,
resembling humans;
the earthen dwarves,
as Durin commanded.

The creation of humans

Then came three gods
from the clan of the Aesir,[25]
they were mighty and merciful –
they came to the shore.

On the beach they found lying,
they found Ask and Embla,[26]
listless and lifeless –
no spark of life.

Souls they had not,
nor senses either,
no warmth of life,
and no living color.

Odin gave souls to them,
Hönir their senses,
Lodur brought warmth of life
and bright, blooming colors.

---

[23] The meaning of the elder dwarf's name, *Motsognir*, is unknown. These primordial dwarves attempted to create humans. Human-like creatures in earliest times appear in many indigenous myths.

[24] The same applies to the name *Durin*. After these two verses about the first dwarves, there are, in the *Völuspá*, a series of verses giving a genealogy of dwarf names. I have omitted them here.

[25] The three Aesir gods who created humans are *Odin*, *Hönir* and *Lodur*, who are named further below. In other parts of the *Edda*, the three creator brother-gods are listed as *Odin*, *Vili* and *Vé*. Only Odin plays a further, significant role in other mythic texts and poems, including the *Völuspá*.

[26] *Ask* refers to the ash tree, and *Embla* possibly to the elm. This would therefore be a mythos of creating humans from trees.

Der Weltenbaum und die drei Nornen

Ich weiss eine Esche, heisst
Yggdrasill, Odins Pferd.[27]
Des Baumes Blätter
funkeln mit Nässe.

Das ist der Tau
der täglich ins Tal fällt.
Ewig grün steht der Weltbaum,
Urd's Brunnen am Fuss.[28]

Von dort kommen drei Frauen,
vielwissende Weiber,
von dem Gewässer
unter dem Weltbaum.

Urd heisst die eine,
die andre Werdandi,
die dritte heisst Skuld.[29]

Sie schneiden die Stäbe,
bestimmen das Leben
der Menschenkinder,
und legen die Runen.

---

[27] *Yggdrasill*, "Odin's Pferd," der Name des Weltenbaums, deutet auf die Funktion des Baumes als Achse für schamanische Reisen zu oberen und unteren Welten.

[28] *Urd* ist sowohl der Name des Brunnens am Fuss des Baumes (der auch Mimir's Brunnen heisst) als auch einer der Nornen. *Urd* bedeutet Gewebe des Lebens und auch Schicksal oder Geschick, ist also zukünftig.

[29] Der Name *Skuld*, oder *Skjuld*, ist mit "Schuld" und "Schulden" verwandt, bedeutet also das Karma der vergangenen Taten. *Werdandi* ist mit "Werden" verbunden – also was sich gegenwärtig entwickelt.

The World Tree and the Three Norns

An ash-tree I know, called
Yggdrasill, or Odins Horse.[30]
Sparkling moisture
lies on its leaves.

This is the dew, that
drops down in the valley.
Ever green stands the world tree,
Urd's well at its roots.[31]

From there come three maidens,
three women of wisdom,
from the deep waters
at the root of the Tree.

One is called Urd,
Verdandi another,
and Skuld is the third.[32]

They carve into wood,
deciding the lives
of the children of men,
choosing the runes.

---

[30] *Yggdrasill*, or "Odin's Horse," the name of the world tree, points to its function as the axis for shamanic travelling to upper and lower worlds.

[31] *Urd* is the name of the well at the foot of the world tree (also called Mimir's Well) as well as the name of one of the three norns. *Urd* refers to the web of life and to destiny, and thus is future-oriented.

[32] The name *Skuld* relates to words for "guilt" and "debt" and thus is related to the *karma* associated with our past actions. *Werdandi* is related to the German word for "becoming," what is unfolding in the present.

Gullveig die Goldene und der Ursprung des Krieges

Auch das weiss ich noch –
wie der Krieg zuerst kam,
als Götter die Gullveig[33]
die Goldene, stiessen.

Dreimal verbrannten sie
die dreifache Göttin,
in Heervaters Hallen.
Doch lebt sie noch heute.

Heide[34] hiess man sie,
wo ins Hause sie kam;
die weise Seherin,
mit Zauberkünsten.

Den Seidr[35] kannte sie,
auch die Wahrsagerei.
Den widrigen Weibern
brachte sie Wonne.

Zum Richtstuhl gingen
die Heiligen alle,
Rat hielten die Götter
untereinander:

Sollten die Asen
Tribut zuerst zahlen?
Oder sollten sie alle
die Opfer empfangen?[36]

---

[33] Der Name *Gullveig* bedeutet so etwas wie "Kraft des Goldes." Ihre Geschichte soll den Ursprung des Krieges zwischen den eingewanderten Asen und und den einheimischen Wanen, zu denen auch Gullveig gehört, erläutern. In *Brunnen der Erinnerung* deute ich sie so: die Asen haben durch Gier nach Gold die Gullveig angegriffen. Aber sie war eine Göttin mit mächtiger Zauberkraft, und die Wanen verteidigten sich.

[34] *Heide* bedeutet allgemein "Seherin," aber auch die Heide, und so auch Heidin.

[35] *Seidr* ist die Zauberzeremonie der Völvas oder Heidrs.

[36] Der Streit ist geht darum, welche Götter (Asen oder Wanen) zuerst Tribut bezahlt bekommen – also Gold!

Gullveig the Golden and the Origin of War

And this too I know –
how war came to the world,
when Gullveig the Golden[37]
was speared by the skygods.

Three times they burned her,
the thrice-born Goddess,
in the Warfather's hall.
Yet still she lives on.

Heathen[38] they called her,
wherever she wandered;
seeress, sorceress,
in soothsaying trance.

She made seidr[39] magic
wherever she could; and
to contrary women
was always welcome.

Then the Holy Ones
gathered in council seats,
and the sky gods debated
among themselves thus:

Should the Aesir gods
first pay a tribute, or
should all gods equally,
offerings receive?[40]

---

[37] The name *Gullveig* means something like "power of gold." Her story is meant to tell of the origin of the war between the immigrating Aesir gods and the indigenous Vanir deities, of whom Gullveig is one. In *The Well of Remembrance*, I interpret it as follows: the Aesir, motivated by lust for gold, attacked Gullveig. But she was a goddess with powerful magic and the Vanir struck back.

[38] Heathen is another name for seeress, but also the herb, the heath and the heathen pagans.

[39] *Seidr* is the name for the divination ceremonies of the völvas.

[40] The dispute is over which deities (Aesir oder Vanir) should be paid first – i.e. over gold!

Den Speer warf Odin
ins Heer ihrer Gegner -
und so kam zuerst
der Krieg in die Welt.[41]

Es brach die Mauer,
die hohe, von Asgard;
die streitkühnen Wanen
stampften die Flur.

Zum Richtstuhl gingen
die Heiligen alle,
Rat hielten die Götter
untereinander:

Wer hatte die Luft gefüllt
mit Trug und mit Gift?
Wer versprach Freyja
dem Riesen als Weib? [42]

Der Donnergott Thor
hat zornig geschlagen;
der sitzt selten stille,
wenn er solches erfährt.

Jetzt wurden Eide
gebrochen, und Treue,
die bindenden Worte
der Götter vergessen.

---

[41] So fängt der Krieg an: die Asen streiten mit den Wanen um Gold, versuchen erfolglos die Gullveig um-
zubringen und dann wirft Odin den ersten Speer.

[42] Dann kommt ein zweiter Kriegsgrund dazu: der trügerische Anstifter *Loki*, der zu den Asen gehört, hat
einem Riesen die Schönheitsgöttin *Freyja*, die zu den Wanen gehört, versprochen - ohne ihre Erlaubnis.

Odin hurled his spear
at the enemy hosts --
and so for the first time
war came to the world.[43]

The walls of Asgard
were crumbling and crashing;
the Vanir gods raging,
trampled the ground.

Then the Holy Ones
gathered in council seats,
the sky-gods debated
among themselves thus:

Who filled the air
with the stench of betrayal?
Who promised Freyja
as a wife to the giants?[44]

Great Thor the Thunderer
fought fiercely the foe;
this god seldom stays still,
when he hears of such deeds.

Now vows were broken,
and binding agreements.
The gods' solemn oaths
were forgotten again.

---

[43] So this is how the war started: the Aesir argue with the Vanir about gold, unsuccessfully try to kill Gullveig and then Odin throws the first spear.

[44] A second cause of war is added: the treacherous instigator *Loki*, who belongs to the Aesir gods, had promised *Freyja*, the Vanir goddess of love and beauty, to a giant – without her permission,

Mimirs Brunnen, Odins Auge

Ich weiss wo das Horn
des Heimdall verborgen:
unter dem höchsten
und heiligsten Baum.[45]

In schäumendem Sturz
seh' ich Wasser fallen;
von Walvaters Pfand.
Wollt wissen noch mehr?

Allein sass ich, draussen,
zu mir kam der Alte,
der furchtbare Ase,
ins Auge mir sah.

Was fragt Ihr mich jetzt?
Was wollt Ihr von mir?

Odin, ich weiss wo Du
dein Aug' hast verborgen:
in Mimir's wundervollen Brunnen.

Met trinkt der Mimir[46]
an jeglichem Morgen,
aus Walvater's Pfande.
Wollt wissen noch mehr?

Ringe und Halsschmuck
hat Heervater geschenkt,
für mein spähendes Sehen
und Worte der Weisheit.

---

[45] Die Seherin lässt jetzt ihre Schau in die Vergangenheit - Ursprung der Welt, und der Kriege - und
beschreibt die seherische Aufgabe die Odin ihr gestellt hat, in dem er ein Auge in Mimir's Brunnen (auch
Wasserfall) als Pfand gibt. Brunnen, Wasserfall und Heimdall's Horn liegen am Fuss des Weltbaumes
Yggdrasil, der *axis mundi*. Odin erwarb sich durch den Pfand seines Auges das Schauen in die Vergangenheit
und die Zukunft. *Heervater, Walvater, der Ase* - sind alles Benennungen von Odin.

[46] *Mimir*, der Riesengeist des Weltbaumes, der Hüter der Weltachse, ermöglicht das Divinationsschauen in
alle Welten und alle Zeiten. Das Schauen ist verstärkt durch das trinken von visionären Met. Die Seherin
vermittelt die Verbindung und den Dialog zwischen Odin und Mimir.

Mimirs Well, Odins Eye

I know where Heimdall's
horn is hidden:
under that highest and
holiest of trees.[47]

In high-foaming spray
water falling I see,
from the well, with Odin's pledge.
Would you know still more?

Outside I sat, alone,
when the Old One came,
the terrible Aesir God,
and looked in my eye.

For what do you ask?
What seek you from me?

I know, Odin, where
you've hidden your eye:
in Mimir's marvellous well.

Mimir drinks mead,[48]
every day in the morning,
from the well, with Odin's pledge.
Would you know still more?

Necklace and bracelets
this Father God gave me,
for my far-seeing visions
and words of wisdom.

---

[47] The seeress now leaves her stories of the past – origin of the world, origin of the wars – and describes the visionary task that Odin has asked from her, in exchange for his pledging one eye into Mimir's well (also a waterfall). The well, the waterfall and Heimdall's horn are situated at the foot of the world tree Yggdrasil, the *axis mundi*. Through his payment of the pledge of one eye, Odin has gained access to visions of the past and the future.

[48] *Mimir*, the Giant-Spirit of the World Tree, the Keeper of the World-Axis, enables the divinatory seeing into all worlds and all times. The seeing is made more vivid through the drinking of the visionary mead. The seeress mediates the connection and the dialog between Odin and Mimir.

Baldurs Mord, Lokis Bestrafung

Fern schau ich und weit,
durch alle Welten hindurch.

Baldur seh' ich auch,
den blutenden Gott:
Tod war ihm bestimmt,
als des Odin's Sohn.

War hoch gewachsen
unter grünen Bäumen,
der Strauch der Mistel,[49]
so zart und so schön.

Der zierliche Zweig,
scheinbar so harmlos,
wird grässlicher Speer,
von Hödur geschleudert.

Des Baldurs Bruder[50]
wird baldigst geboren;
obwohl nur ein Tag alt,
gelobt er die Rache.

Nicht wäscht er die Hände,
noch kämmt' er das Haar,
eh' des Baldur's Töter
zur Hel wird gebracht.

Es beweint die Frigg
im wässrigen Saale,
das Unglück Walhallas.
Wollt wissen noch mehr?

---

[49] *Baldur's* Mutter *Frigga* hatte von allen Bäumen und Pflanzen ein Gelübde gewonnen, in den Kampfspielen der Asen den geliebten Sohn nicht zu verletzen – hatte aber die schmächtige Mistel nicht beachtet. Der listige Loki hat dieses Versehen ausgebeutet, indem er einen Mistelzweig in einen Speer verwandelt, und *Hödur*, dem blinden Bruder Baldur's, in die Hand drückt. Dieser unbewusste Brudermord ist der Auslöser für den Untergang der Weltordnung.

[50] *Vali*, ein weiterer Sohn Odin's, mit einer Riesin erzeugt, kommt schnell in die Welt, um Baldur's Mord zu rächen.

Balders Murder, Lokis Punishment

Far and wide do I see,
throughout all of the worlds.

Now Balder I see,
the god who is bleeding.
His doom was determined,
as great Odin's son.

Growing slender and tall
among the green trees,
is the mistletoe shrub,[51]
so tender and fair.

That fragile sprig,
so seemingly harmless,
was horrible weapon
when hurled by Hödur.

Now Balder's brother[52]
is born soon thereafter;
though but one day old,
he vows his vengeance.

His hands he washes not,
and his hair he combs not,
till Balder's murderer
is sent off to Hel.

Fair Frigga does weep
in her watery home,
for Valhalla's misfortune.
Would you know still more?

---

[51] *Balder's* mother *Frigga* had persuaded all trees and plants not to be part of any harm to her beloved son, in the combat games the Aesir liked to play – but she had overlooked the seemingly fragile mistletoe. The cunning Loki exploited this oversight – turning a twig of mistle into a spear, and putting it into the hands of *Hödur*, Balder's blind brother. This unconscious fratricide is the catalyst for the collapse of the world order.

[52] *Vali*, another son of Odin and a Giantess, is born and grows up very quickly, vowing to take revenge for Balder's murder.

Gefesselt seh' ich,
bei kochenden Quellen:
des listigen Lokis[53]
elenden Leib.

Dort sitzt auch Sigyn,
sein unglückliches Weib,
mit grimmiger Miene.
Wollt wissen noch mehr?

Hel - Land der Toten

Ein Fluss fliest im Osten
durch vergiftetes Land,[54]
von schneidender Kälte;
ist Schreckstrom genannt.

Dort seh' ich waten
durch reissende Strömung
Verräter und Mörderer,
auch Brecher der Ehe.

Dort seh' ich Nidhöggr,[55]
Blut trinkend, Leichen
fressendes Ungeheuer.
Wollt wissen noch mehr?

Einen Saal seh' ich auch,
so fern von der Sonne,
am Strande der Toten,
die Tore zum Norden.

---

[53] In dieser Geschichte agiert der listige Trickster Loki als Feind der Götter (obwohl er in anderen Geschichten den Göttern hilft): er stiftet den Mord von Baldur an, was dann zum *Ragnarök* führt. Zur Bestrafung wird er von den Asen gefesselt (wie Prometheus); die Gifttropfen einer Schlange werden von seiner Frau *Sigyn* in einer Schale aufgenommen, anstatt in sein Gesicht zu fallen.

[54] Ist das nur eine mythische Vorstellung oder bezieht sich die Vision des vergifteten Landes im Osten auf die Ukrainische Stadt Tschernobyl in der Nähe des Flusses Pripyat, von Radioaktivität vergiftet im 20. Jahrhundert?

[55] *Nidhöggr* heisst der Totendrache, der Menschenkörper verzehrt im Reich des Todes. An anderer Stelle ist er die Risenschlange die an den Wurzeln des Weltbaumes nagt, bis er zerbricht.

A prisoner I see
by the boiling springs:
the treacherous Lokis[56]
miserable form.

There too sits Sigyn,
his unfortunate wife,
with woeful demeanor.
Would you know still more?

Hel - Land of the Dead

From the East flows a stream
through poisonous lands,[57]
cutting sharply with cold;
called river of terror.

Waist-deep wading
through watery torrents,
are traitors and murderers,
and adulterers too.

There I see Nidhöggr[58]
drink blood from the corpses,
that man-eating monster.
Would you know still more?

A dwelling I see,
far away from the sun,
near the land of the dead,
its gates to the North.

---

[56] In this story, the cunning trickster Loki acts as enemy of the gods (although in others he helps them): he is the instigator of Balders murder, which in the end leads to the *ragnarök*. As punishment, the Aesir gods bind him to a rock (like Prometheus); the drops from a venomous snake are collected by his wife *Sigyn*, instead of falling on to his face.

[57] Is this only a mythic conception, or could the vision of poisoned lands in the East refer to the Ukrainian town of Chernobyl, poisoned by radioactivity in the 20th century, near the Pripyat River?

[58] *Nidhöggr* is the name of the death dragon that devours human corpses. Elsewhere it is the name of the giant serpent, gnawing at the roots of the World Tree, until it breaks apart.

Vergiftete Tropfen
fallen hier durch das Dach.[59]
Von Schlangenleibern ist
umwunden der Saal.

Ragnarök - Weltuntergang

Im Osten die Alte,
sitzt im eisernen Wald;
sie gebiert dort Fenrirs[60]
furchtbare Brut.

Von diesen allen,
wird's einer dann sein,
der in Trollengestalt,
die Sonne verschlingt.[61]

Fenrir füllt sich mit Fleisch
der gefallenen Krieger;
mit Blut ganz bespritzt
wird der Götter Sitz.

Schwarz scheint die Sonne
die Sommer darauf;
es gibt wütendes Wetter.
Wollt wissen noch mehr?

Laut heult der Wolf
vor seiner Höhle;
er reisst los seine Fessel,
und jetzt läuft er frei.

---

[59] In *Brunnen der Erinnerung* habe ich die Visionen der *Völuspa* mit erdgeschichtlichen Katastrophen im späten Mittelalter und im 20. Jahrhundert in Verbindung gebracht. "Vergiftete Tropfen vom Dach" bezieht sich vielleicht auf Vulkanausbrüche und auf industriellen "sauren Regen."

[60] *Fenrir*, oder *Fenriswolf*, ist das Ungeheuer, dessen Brut die Weltzerstörung herbeibringt. Symbolisch bedeutet er die gefrässige Gier und Aggression, die die Ausbeutung und Zerstörung unserer Biosphäre antreiben.

[61] Die Trollengestalt, die die Sonne verschlingt, bezieht sich vielleicht auf die gigantischen Wolkenbäume aus schwarzer Vulkanasche, die die Sonne manchmal mehrere Jahre lang verdunkelt haben, z.B. in Island.

Here poisonous drops
drip from the roof.[62]
and coils of serpents
encircle the walls.

Ragnarök - Collapse of the World

In the East an old hag
sits in the iron forest;
there she bears Fenrir's[63]
terrible brood.

One among these,
will one of these days,
in the form of a troll,
swallow the sun.[64]

Fenrir feeds on the flesh
of fallen warriors,
spattering with blood
the seat of the gods.

The sun is turned black
in the summers thereafter;
continuing violent weather.
Would you know still more?

Loud howls the wolf
at the mouth of his cave;
he tears off his fetters,
and now he runs free.

---

[62] In *The Well of Remembrance* I related the prophecies of the *Völuspa* with cataclysmic earth changes in the late Middle Ages and in the 20th century. "Poisonous drops from the roof" refer perhaps to volcanic eruptions and to industrial "acid rain."

[63] *Fenrir* or *Fenriswolf* is the monster whose offspring bring about the destruction of the world. Symbolically, it is the voracious greed and aggression that fuels the runaway exploitation and destruction of our biosphere.

[64] The troll that devours the sun perhaps refers to the massive clouds of black volcanic ash that sometimes have darkenend the sun for years, e.g. in Iceland.

Vieles weiss ich,
weithin seh ich,
der siegreichen Götter
schrecklich Geschick.

Brüder schlagen und morden einander,
Geschwistersöhne
zerbrechen die Sippe.
Wüst ist's in der Welt,
Untreue gibt's auch.

Beilzeit, Schwertzeit
zerschmetterte Schilde;
Windzeit, Wolfzeit,
bis Einsturz der Welt.

Niemand will mehr
die anderen schonen.
Das glänzende Gjallarhorn
verkündet das Ende.

Hell bläst Heimdall
hochhebend das Horn.
Und Odin murmelt
mit Mimir's Haupt.[65]

Der Yggdrasil zittert,[66]
es braust die ragende Esche;
der Riese kommt los,[67]
es bebt in der Unterwelt;
und der feurige Riese[68]
verschlingt den Baum.

---

[65] Mimir ist der Weltbaumriese, der Hüter der Achse, der Erinnerer, dessen Name mit lat. *memor* verwandt ist. Nachdem er enthauptet wurde, bewahrt Odin seinen Schädel und benützt ihn zum Weissagen, wie es bei Asiatischen Schamanen auch üblich war.

[66] Der Baum Yggdrasil ist die Weltachse – wenn also der Weltbaum zittert, kommt die ganze Erde ins Beben.

[67] Der unterirdische Riese ist der Fenriswolf – wenn er von seinen Fesseln loskommt, gibt es Erdbeben.

[68] Der feurige Riese, auch *Surt* genannt, verbrennt die Wälder – wie in Russland im Jahr 2010.

Much do I know,
far distant I see,
The conquering gods'
Terrible fate.

Brothers do battle and murder each other,
the sons of siblings
break bonds of clan.
Much woe's in the world,
and treachery too.

It's axe-time, sword-time,
time of shattered shields;
wind-time, wolf-time,
till the world breaks down.

No one any more
considers the others.
The gleaming Gjallarhorn
announces the end.

Loud blows Heimdall,
he lifts high the horn.
And Odin murmurs,
with Mimir's head.[69]

Yggdrasil trembles,
the towering ash groans;[70]
the giant is loosened,
the underworld quakes;[71]
the flaming giant[72]
devours the trees.

---

[69] Mimir is the giant spirit of the world tree, the Rememberer, the Keeper of the Axis, whose name is related to the lat. *memor*. After he was decapitated, Odin preserved his skull and used it for oracular purposes, as was also the custom among some Asiatic shamans.

[70] The Yggdrasil tree is the World Axis – thus when it trembles, the whole Earth starts shaking.

[71] The giant in the underworld is the Fenriswolf – when he breaks out of his fetters, we get earthquakes.

[72] The flaming, fiery giant, elswhere called *Surt*, burns the forests – as in Russia in 2010.

Wie gehts bei den Asen?
Wie steht's bei den Alben?
Ganz Riesenheim dröhnt,
zum Rat gehn die Götter.

Die Zwerge stöhnen
vor steinernen Toren,
die Weisen der Felsen.
Wollt wissen noch mehr?

Laut heult der Wolf
vor seiner Höhle;
er reisst seine Fessel,
es rennt der Wolf.

Vieles weiss ich,
weithin seh ich,
der siegreichen Götter
schrecklich Geschick.

Von Osten ein Riese,
hoch hebt er sein Schild.
Die Midgardschlange[73]
windet sich wütend,

und schlägt die Wellen.
Es kreischt der Adler.
Mit zerrissenen Leichen
das Totenschiff kommt.

---

[73] Die sich windende, wütende Schlage bedeutet das Überfluten der Flüsse, und auch die Riesenwellen (*Tsunami*) des Meeres.

What ails the Aesir?
What troubles the elves?
The giants are roaring,
The gods meet in council.

The gnomes are groaning,
by their gates of rock,
the wise spirits of stone.
Would you know still more?

Loud howls the wolf
at the mouth of his cave;
he tears off his fetters,
and now he runs free.

This much do I know,
far-distant I see,
the conquering gods'
terrible fate.

From the East comes a giant,
his shield he holds high.
The Midgard serpent coils[74]
as raging rivers wind,

and whip up the waves.
The eagle screams on high.
With torn-up corpses,
the deathship comes.

---

[74] The raging, winding serpent signifies both the flooding of the rivers and the gigantic *tsunami* ocean waves.

Die Riesen kommen,
in wilden Horden.
Das Wolf Ungeheuer,
und der Loki auch.

Von Süden kommt Surt,[75]
Versenger der Pflanzen;
sein feuriges Schwert
brennt wie die Sonne.

Es zerbrechen die Berge,
die Trollweiber taumeln,[76]
zu Hel fahren Menschen,
der Himmel zerspringt.

Odin's Frau Frigga,[77]
geschieht noch ein Leid,
da Odin jetzt los zieht,
den Wolf zu bekämpfen.

Freyr, der Riesenfeind,
gegen Surt muss fechten.
Der Geliebte der Frigg
fällt leblos im Kampf.[78]

Dann kommt der Starke,
Widar, der Odinssohn;
den Wolf bekämpft er.
Er stösst das Schwert
durch gähnenden Rachen—
so rächt er den Vater.

---

[75] *Surt* ist der Feuerriese, dessen versengender Brand vom Süden die Erde verbrennt - was wir "globale Hitze" nennen.

[76] *Trolle* sind haarige, hässliche Riesenweiber, den Menschen feindlich und schädlich gesinnt.

[77] Friggas erstes Leid war ihren Sohn, Baldur, zu verlieren; jetzt wird auch Odin sterben.

[78] Die Götter kämpfen gegen die welt-zerstörenden Ungeheuer: Odin gegen den Fenriswolf, unterliegt ihm aber; wird dann durch seinen Sohn *Widar* gerächt; Freyr kämpft gegen Surt.

The giants are coming,
in horrible hordes.
And the monstrous Wolf,
even Loki as well.

From the South comes Surt,[79]
who scorches the plants;
his flaming sword
burns hot as the sun.

The mountains are cracking,
the trollwomen reeling,[80]
to Hel go the humans,
the heavens rupture.

For Odin's wife Frigga,[81]
a second great grief,
as Odin goes forth now,
to fight Fenriswolf.

Freyr the giant-slayer
does battle with Surt.
Frigga's beloved
is felled in the fight.[82]

Here comes the strong one,
Odin's son Widar,
to battle the great Wolf.
He thrusts his sword
through its gaping jaws—
thus is Odin avenged.

---

[79] *Surt* is the fire-giant, whose flaming heat, coming from the South, scorches the Earth - the slow-motion catastrophe we call "global warming."

[80] *Trolls* are ugly, hairy female giants, who are hostile and dangerous to humans.

[81] Frigga's first loss was her son Balder; now her husband, Odin will also die.

[82] The gods are fighting against the world-destroying monsters: Odin battles the Fenriswolf, but is defeated, and then avenged by his son *Widar;* Freyr fights against Surt.

Nun kommt noch einer:
Thor, Sohn der Erde;
der mächtige Krieger,
bekämpft die Schlange.

Der Wächter von Midgard,
er schlägt zu mit Wut.
Beängstigte Menschen
verlassen ihr Haus.

Schwarz wird die Sonne,
das Land sinkt ins Meer
vom Himmel stürzen
die strahlenden Sterne.

Das Feuer umtost
den allnährenden Baum;
die sengende Hitze
steigt hoch zum Himmel.[83]

Laut heult der Wolf
vor seiner Höhle;
er reisst seine Fessel,
es rennt der Wolf.

Vieles weiss ich,
weithin seh ich,
der siegreichen Götter
schrecklich Geschick.

---

[83] Vielleicht ist das eine vorausschauende Vision vom fieberhaften Anheizen der Erde im 20. Jahrhundert, dem sogenannten *Treibhauseffekt*.

Now comes another:
Thor, son of Earth;
this mighty warrior
battles the Serpent.

Protector of Midgard,
he fights with fierce rage.
Terrified people
are fleeing their homes.

The sun turns black,
land sinks into sea,
and the radiant stars
fall from the sky.

Hot flames engulf
the all-nourishing tree;
the searing heat rises
high in the heavens. [84]

Loud howls the wolf
at the mouth of his cave;
he tears off his fetters,
and now he runs free.

Much do I know,
far-distant I see,
the conquering gods'
terrible fate.

---

[84] Perhaps this is a premonitory vision of the Earth's feverish over-heating in the 20th century, the so-called *greenhouse effect*.

Auferstehung der Grünen Erde

Aufsteigen seh' ich
zum anderen Male
aus den Fluten die Erde,
und wieder ergrünen.

Es schäumen Gewässer.
Hoch über den Bergen
schwebt der Adler,
und jagt die Fische.

Am Ida-feld[85] seh' ich
die Asen sich finden;
reden dort miteinander
von der schrecklichen Schlange.

Sie denken zurück
ans gewaltige Ende;
an die uralten Runen,
Gottvaters Geheimniss.

Im Grase liegen,
finden sie wieder
die wundersamen goldenen Tafeln,[86]
die sie schon hatten
in ältester Zeit.

Ganz unbesät werden
hochwachsen die Äcker.[87]
Es heilt alles Unheil,
und Balder kehrt heim.

---

[85] Das Ida-Feld ist die überirdische, "glänzende Ebene," wo die Götter sich befanden vor der Schöpfung der Menschen; und hier wieder nach dem Ragnarök.

[86] Die goldenen Tafeln, mit göttlichen Anweisungen, hatten sie gefunden am Anfang der Schöpfung; und jetzt wieder, bei einem neuen Schöpfungszyklus.

[87] Eine Vision von der spontaner Erneuerung der Erde, durch Baldur dem grünen Vegetationsgott.

Resurrection of the Green Earth

I see the Earth,
rising up from below,
out of the floods,
with all greening plants.

Falling waters foam.
High over the mountains
flies the eagle,
hunting for fish.

I see the Aesir gods meet
on the field of Ida,[88]
and speak with each other
of the terrible serpent.

They remember the great
and awesome end-time,
and ancient rune secrets
of the High Father-God.

Lying in the grass,
they find them again,
the wonderful golden tablets,[89]
as they had them before,
in ancient times.

Without being sown,
the fields will grow high.[90]
All harm will be healed,
as Balder comes back.

---

[88] The "field of Ida" is the otherworldly, "shining plain," on which the gods found themselves before the creation of human beings; and here again now, after the ragnarök.

[89] The golden tablets, with divine instructions, were found at the beginning of the creation; and here again, at the start of a new cycle of creation.

[90] Here is a vision of the spontaneous regeneration of the Earth, through Balder the green vegetation deity.

Hödur[91] und Balder
wohnen wieder
in den heiligen Hallen.
Wollt wissen noch mehr?

Dann wird der Hönir[92]
die Losstäbe legen.
Die Söhne der Brüder
wohnen in Windheim.

Jetzt seh' ich einen Saal,
der glänzt wie die Sonne,
mit rot-gold bedeckt;
Gimlé[93] ist sein Name.

Dort sollen die Scharen
der Treuen wohnen,
und ohne Schuld das Leben
auf ewig geniessen.

Von oben herab,
zum Rat der Götter,
kommt jetzt der Mächtige,[94]
der alles beherrscht.

Der dunkle Todesdrache
fliegt von unten hinauf;
in den Flügeln trägt er
die Leichen der Menschen.

Und dann...sinkt er nach unten.

---

[91] Hödur ist der blinde Brüder Baldurs, der durch eine von Loki geleitete Mistel den Baldur umgebracht hat; hier aber sind die zwei Brüder die Erben der Asengötter. Laut Rudolf Steiner symbolisiert Baldur die Weisheit und Hödur die Blindheit – Unbewusstheit (Hödur) hat die Weisheit (Baldur) getötet. Nach dem Weltuntergang sind beide wieder auf der Erde, mit ihren Söhnen.

[92] Hönir ist ein weiterer Asengott, über den sehr wenig geschrieben ist; er war an der Schöpfung der Menschen beteiligt, indem er diesen den Verstand gegeben hat.

[93] *Gimlé* ist ein goldener Saal, der vom Feuer nicht berührt werden kann; also ein paradiesischer Ort, in dem die tugendsamen Gestorbenen sich befinden.

[94] Manche meinen "der Mächtige" bezieht sich auf Christus, dessen Lehren im 10. Jahrhundert in den nordischen Ländern angekommen sind.

Hödur[95] and Balder
will dwell once again
in the holy halls of the gods.
Would you know still more?

Then Hönir[96] will handle
the rods for divining.
The sons of both brothers
dwell in the Winds' Home.

Now a hall I see
more bright than the sun,
with a red-golden roof;
Gimlé[97] is its name.

There dwell the noble
and kind ones forever,
their lives free of guilt, and
in gracious ease.

Down from above,
to the council of gods,
the mighty Lord[98] comes,
and rules over all.

The dark dragon of death
flies up from below;
in his wings he carries
the corpses of men.

And now...he sinks down.

---

[95] Hödur is the blind brother of Balder who, through Loki's treachery, threw the mistletoe branch
that killed Balder; here they are the two brothers who inherit the realm of the Aesir gods. According to
Rudolf Steiner, Balder symbolizes wisdom and Hödur blindness – unconsciousness (Hödur) has killed
wisdom (Balder); both will be present again after the collapse of the world, with their sons.

[96] Hönir is another Aesir god about whom very little is written; he was present at the creation of hu-
man beings, and provided them with the faculty of understanding.

[97] *Gimlé* is a golden hall that can't be touched by fire; that means it is an otherworldly place, in which
the virtuous deceased may find themselves.

[98] Some commentators believe the "Lord" refers to Christ, whose teachings arrived in the Nordic lands
around the 10th century.

Aus dem Wafthrúdnismal[99]

Woher kommt zum glatten Himmel
die Sonne, wenn der Wolf sie verschlungen hat?

Eine Tochter entstammt
der strahlenden Göttin
wenn der Wolf sie verschlingt.
Glänzend fährt sie auf den Bahnen der Mutter[100]
nach dem Fallen der Götter.

Wer sind die Mädchen[101]
voll Weisheit und Sinn,
die wir schweben sehen
weithin übers Meer?

Drei Scharen von Mädchen,
Töchter der Riesen,
fahren hinab zu den Dörfern.[102]
Sind Beschützer der Menschen,
doch sie leben bei Riesen.

---

[99] Diese Verse aus dem *Wafthrúdismal*, ein weiteres Eddalied, ergänzen die Beschreibung der Szene nach dem Ragnarök. Die Form ist auch ein Dialog: Odin befragt den weisen Riesen *Wafthrúdnir*. Ein Weltzyklus geht zu Ende, ein neuer beginnt.

[100] Nachdem die Sonne durch eine Vulkanwolke (Wolf) verschlungen wurde, war sie unsichtbar für eine Zeit – und erschien dann wieder, als "Tochter," auf der gewohnten Kreislaufbahn.

[101] Sind das vielleicht die Geister der Wale und Delphine, mit denen die Menschen in der neuen Zeit ein tiefere Verbindung haben werden?

[102] Die weisen Riesinnen erinnern an die drei "mächtigen Frauen," die in den ersten Versen der *Völuspá* erscheinen. In ihrer Funktion als Schutzgeister für die Menschen, indem sie in die Dörfer kommen, ähneln sie den Fruchtbarkeitsgeistern (*Disen*), die in den Landwirtschaft und Gartenbau betreibenden Dörfern eine Rolle spielten. Diese Verse deuten auf eine Wiederherstellung alter Göttinnenkulte – Kulte für die Sonnengöttin, und den Schutz der Gewässer und des Landes.

From the Vafthrúdnismal[103]

Whence comes the sun in the smooth sky,
after the Wolf has devoured her?

The sun had a daughter,
when Wolf had devoured her.
This radiant maiden will ride
on the paths of her mother,[104]
after the fall of the gods.

Who are the maidens[105]
of wisdom and sense,
that we see hovering
over the wide seas?

Three throngs of maidens,
daughters of giants,
descend on the villages.[106]
They're protectors of humans,
yet they live with the giants.

---

[103] These verses from the *Vafthrúdismal*, another song from the *Edda*, amplify the description of the scene after the ragnarök. It is also in the form of a dialog: Odin is questioning the wise giant *Vafthrúdnir*. One world cycle is ending, another one is beginning.

[104] After the sun had been devoured by a volcanic ash-cloud, it became invisible for a time – and later reappeared, as her "daughter," moving in the same orbital pathway.

[105] Does this perhaps refer to the spirits of whales and dolphins, with whom humans in the coming age will have deeper alliances of understanding?

[106] The wise giant maidens remind us of the three "mighty women," who appeared in the early part of the *Völuspá*. In their functioning as protective spirits for humans, coming in to the villages, they remind of the *disir* – land spirits that furthered the fertility of the gardening and farming villages. These verses point to a resurrection of the ancient goddess cults of the sun *(Sunna)*, the earth and the waters.

Hildegard von Bingen[1]
Die dreifache Natur des Menschen

Drei Pfade hat der Mensch in sich, in denen sich sein Leben tätigt:
die Seele, den Leib und die Sinne.

Die Seele belebt den Leib
und leitet den Lebenshauch auch in die Sinne.

Der Leib zieht die Seele an sich
und öffnet die Sinne (nach aussen).

Die Sinne endlich berühren die Seele
und vermitteln dem Körper die Reize (der Sinneswelt).

Wie das Licht sich in die Finsternis ergiesst,
so gibt die Seele dem Körper das Leben.

Zwei Hauptkräfte hat sie, gleich zwei Armen: Erkenntnis und Wille.

Nicht als ob die Seele dieser Kräfte bedürfte, um sich zu bewegen.
Sie offenbart sich in diesen Kräften wie die Sonne in ihrem Glanze.

---

[1] Hildegard von Bingen (1098-1179). Dieser Text ist aus ihrem ersten Buch von Gesichten: *Scivias – Wisse die Wege.*

Hildegard von Bingen[2]
The threefold nature of the human being

The human being has three pathways, in which life's activities take place:
the soul, the body and the senses.

The soul animates the body
and brings the breath of life into the senses.

The body draws the soul to itself
and opens the senses (to the exterior world).

The senses touch the soul
and convey the stimuli (of the sense world) to the body.

Just as light pours itself into the darkness
so does the soul pour itself in to the body.

The soul has two main powers, like two arms: knowledge and will.

Not that the soul needs these arms in order to move or function.
It manifests itself in these powers, just as the Sun does in its radiance.

---

[2]   Hildegard von Bingen (1098-1179). This passage is from her first book of visions: *Scivias – Know the Ways*.

Die höchste feurige Kraft[3]

Die höchste feurige Kraft hat jedweden Funken des Leben entzündet,
und nichts Tödliches sprüht aus von dieser Kraft.
Sie bestimmt alle Wirklichkeit.

Mit den höheren Flügeln umfliegt diese Kraft den Erdkreis: mit
Weisheit hat sie das All geordnet.

Das feurige Leben göttlicher Wesenheit zündet an die Schönheiten der
Fluren, leuchtet über den Gewässern und brennt in Sonne, Mond und
Sternen.

Mit jedem unsichtbaren Lufthauch wird alles zum Leben erweckt.

Sie ruht in aller Wirklichkeit, verborgen als feurige Kraft.

Sie brennt durch alles, so wie der Atem den Menschen unablässig
bewegt, und gleich der windbewegten Flamme im Feuer.

Alles lebt in seiner Wesenheit, und ist kein Tod darin.
Denn *ich bin* dieses Leben.

---

[3] Aus: *De operatione Dei.* Übertragen als: *Welt und Mensch.*

The highest fiery force [4]

The highest fiery force has ignited the spark in every form of life –
nothing of death comes from this force.
It determines all actuality.

With higher wings, it encircles the Earth: the order of the cosmos
has been established in wisdom.

The fiery life of divine essence ignites the divine beauty of the fields
of nature, illuminates the waters of Earth and burns in the Sun, the
Moon and the stars.

With every invisible breath of air, everything is awakened to life.

This power rests in all actuality, hidden as fiery force.

It burns throughout everything, like the breath unceasingly moving
in us, and like the wind-blown flames in the fire.

Everything lives in its essence and without any dying.
For *I am* this life.

---

[4] From the book: *De operatione Dei*. Published in a German translation as *Welt und Mensch*.

Nobilissima Viriditas[5]

O edelste Grüne Kraft,

verwurzelt in der Sonne,

erstrahlend im Glanz

über dem Rad (des Lebens).

Kein weltlicher Sinn kann dich begreifen.

Du bist umfangen

von den Armen des göttlichen Geheimnisses.

Du leuchtest wie die Morgenröte

Und brennst wie die Macht der Sonne.

---

[5] Die Visionen und Lehren der Hildegard von Bingen sind in unserer Zeit von erstaunlicher Relevanz und Bedeutung. Ihr Begriff des "Grünen" (*Viriditas*), als der sich in der Schöpfung manifestierender Geist, sowie ihre Lehren über das Göttliche Mutterprinzip sind Vorläufer eines Ökofeminismus und einer zum Christentum gehörenden Schöpfungsspiritualität.

Nobilissima Viriditas[6]

O most noble greenness,

rooted in the Sun,

shining forth in splendor

upon the wheel (of life).

No earthly sense can comprehend you.

You are embraced

by the arms of divine mystery.

You are glowing as the dawn

and burning with the power of the Sun.

---

[6] The visions and teachings of Hildegard von Bingen are of stunning relevance and significance to our time. Her concept of *viriditas* as Spirit manifest in the creation and her emphasis on the Divine Mother principle are forerunners of an ecofeminist, creation spirituality that yet remains within Christianity.

Francesco d'Assisi

Gesang des Bruders Sonne oder Loblied der Geschöpfe[1]

Du Höchster, allvermögender, guter Herr,
  Dein sind die Preisungen, die Herrlichkeit, die Ehre und alle Segnung,
Dir allein, Höchster, kommen sie zu.
Kein Mensch ist würdig, Dich zu nennen.

Gelobet seist Du, mein Herr, mit allen Deinen Geschöpfen,
  besonders unserem edlen Bruder Sonne,
  welcher der Tag ist und uns erhellt durch sich selbst.
Schön ist er und strahlend mit grossem Glanz,
  von Dir Höchster, trägt er das Sinnbild.

Gelobet seist Du, mein Herr, durch Schwester Mond,
  und die Sterne, die Du am Himmel gemacht hast:
  klar, kostbar und schön.

Gelobet seist Du, mein Herr, durch Bruder Wind,
  und durch die Luft und alles Wetter, bewölkt und klar,
  durch den Du Deinen Geschöpfen gibst den Unterhalt.

Gelobet seist Du, mein Herr, durch Schwester Wasser,
  die sehr brauchbar und demütig ist,
  und kostbar und keusch.

---

[1] Franceso d'Assisi (1181-1226) hat diese Loblied komponiert als er krank lag, kurz vor seinem Tode.
Das Lied war auf Italienisch schriebgen, trug aber den Lateinishen Titel – *Canticum Fratris Solis vel Laudes Creatorum*. Es hatte auch eine erste Zeile, auch auf Latein – "Hier beginnt der Lobgesang der Geschöpfe, den der gesegnete Franziskus geschrieben hat, als er krank lag in Dammiano." Franziskus soll den Wunsch ausgedrückt haben, dass Brüder Pacifico, ein ehemaliger Troubadour wie er selbst, diese Lied auf aller Welt singen sollte.

Francesco d'Assisi

The Canticle of Brother Sun or Praises of the Creation[2]

Most high, omnipotent good Lord:
  to You are due praise, glory, honor and all blessings.
  to You, Most High, and You alone.
No humans are worthy to speak Your name.

Be praised, my Lord, with all your creations,
  especially our noble Brother Sun,
  he who is the day, and shines from within himself.
He is most fair and radiant with great splendor,
  of You, Most High, he is the very image.

Be praised, my Lord, by Sister Moon,
  and all the stars that you created in the heavens,
  in clarity, in grace and beauty.

Be praised, my Lord, by Brother Wind,
  and for the air at all times, both cloudy and serene;
  through him you offer sustenance to all your creatures.

Be praised, my Lord, by Sister Water,
  who is most useful and humble,
  and also precious and pure.

---

[2] Francesco d'Assisi (1181-1226) composed this song of praise shortly before he died. The poem was composed in Italian, but its title, in Latin, was – *Canticum Fratris Solis vel Laudes Creatorum.* There was an introductory line, also in Latin – "Here begins the praise song of the creatures, which the blessed Francis composed when he was lying ill in Damiano." Francis is to have expressed the wish that Brother Pacifico, a former troubadour like himself, would sing this song throughout the world.

Gelobet seist Du, mein Herr, durch Bruder Feuer,
  durch ihn erleuchtest Du die Nacht,
  und er ist schön und freudig, und auch robust und stark.

Gelobet seist Du, mein Herr, durch unsere Schwester Mutter Erde,
  die uns ernährt und versorgt,
  vielartige Früchte hervorbringt, mit bunten Blumen und Kräutern.

Gelobet seist Du, mein Herr, durch jene, die verzeihen, und
  durch deine Liebe ertragen Krankheit und Trübsal.

Gesegnet sind Jene, die solches Leid ertragen in Frieden,
  denn von Dir, Höchster, werden sie gekrönt.

Gelobet seist Du, mein Herr, durch unsere Schwester
  Tod des Leibes, welcher kein lebender Mensch entrinnen kann.
  Wehe denen, die in der Todessünde sterben.

Gesegnet sind Jene, die durch Deinen heiligen Willen,
  kein Übel finden in ihrem zweiten Tod.

Gelobt und gesegnet sei mein Herr,
  mit Dankbarkeit dienen wir Dir und grosser Demut.

Be praised, my Lord, by Brother Fire,
  through whom you illuminate the darkness;
  truly he is most fair and joyous, and so robust and strong.

Be praised, my Lord, by Sister Mother Earth,
  who nourishes and sustains us,
  bringing forth all kinds of foods, flowers and green herbs.

Be praised, my Lord, by those who can forgive, and
  through Your love, endure sickness and suffering.

Blesséd are those who suffer who suffer peacefully,
  by you, Most High, they will be crowned.

Be praised, my Lord, for our Sister death of body,
  from whom noone alive escapes.
  Woe betides those who die in mortal sin.

Blesséd are those who find that in Your Holy Will,
  dying the second death shall bring no ill.

All praise and blessings to You, my Lord,
  With gratitude we serve you and humility.

Meister Eckhart[1]

Gott ist allzeit bereit, wir aber sind unbereit.

Gott ist allzeit bereit, wir aber sind unbereit.
Gott ist uns nahe, wir aber sind ihm fern.
Gott ist innen, wir aber sind draussen.
Gott ist in uns daheim, wir aber sind in der Fremde.

Dass ein Mensch ein ruhiges Leben in Gott hat,
das ist gut.

Dass ein Mensch ein mühevolles Leben mit Geduld erträgt,
das ist besser.

Dass man aber Ruhe hat im mühevollen Leben,
das ist das Beste.

---

[1] Meister Eckhart (1260-1327). Diese Texte sind ausgewählt aus seinen Predigen. Was ich an dem Dominikaner Eckhart schätze ist, dass er die streng intellektuelle Atmosphäre der theologischen Schulen, wo alles Lehren und Schreiben auf Latein vorging, verlassen hat. Er wurde ein wandernder Prediger und Seelsorger, der zu den gewöhnlichen Leuten auf Deutsch sprach, und seine mystische Einsichten an der Frage ausrichtete, wie man ein vom Göttlichen inspiriertes Leben führt. Eckhart's Sprache bewirkt ihren Eindruck durch seine fast poetischen, mit Sinn und Einsicht verdichteten Phrasen.

Meister Eckhart[2]

God is always ready, but we are not ready

God is always ready, but we are not ready.
God is near to us, but we are distant from God.
God is within, but we are on the outside.
God is at home in us, but we are in a foreign place.

To lead a peaceful life at one with God,
that is good.

To endure an arduous life with patience,
that is better.

To be at peace in an arduous life,
that is the best.

---

[2] Meister Eckhart (1260-1327). These passages are selected from his published sermons. What I appreciate about the Dominican priest Eckhart is that he emerged from the strict intellectual atmosphere of the theological colleges, with its discourses in Latin, to become an itinerant preacher, speaking to ordinary people in German, applying his mystical insights to the challenges of living a life inspired by divinity. His sermons owe much of their powerful impact to the way he condenses complex thoughts into short colorful phrases that are close to poetry. In German the word for poetry, *Dichtung,* is an alchemical metaphor; it literally means "condensation." Eckhart's poetic sentences are densely packed with insight and meaning.

Ich bitte Gott, dass er mich Gottes quitt mache.

Ich bitte Gott, dass er mich Gottes quitt mache.

In jenem Sein Gottes nämlich, wo Gott über allem Sein und über aller Unterschiedenheit ist, dort war ich selber, da wollte ich mich selber und erkannte mich selber, diesen Menschen, mich zu schaffen.

Darum bin ich Ursache meiner selbst, meinem Sein nach, das ewig ist; nicht aber meinem Werden nach, das zeitlich ist.

Nach der Weise meiner Ungeborenheit, kann ich niemals sterben, bin ich ewig gewesen, bin ich jetzt und werde ich ewig bleiben.

Was ich meiner Geburt nach bin, das wird sterben und zunichtewerden, denn es ist sterblich; darum muss es mit der Zeit vergehen.

Wer diese Rede nicht versteht, der bekümmere sein Herz nicht damit. Denn es ist eine unverhüllte Wahrheit, die da gekommen ist aus dem Herzen Gottes unmittelbar.

I am asking God that I can be done with "God."

I am asking God that I can be done with "God."

For in that beingness of God, in which God is beyond all being and beyond all differences, there I was, and there I willed myself and recognized myself, and brought my self, this human being, into existence.

Therefore I am the prime cause of my self, of my being – that is eternal; but not of my becoming – that is temporal.

In this way, since I am unborn, I can never die. Being unborn, I have always been, I am now, and I will always be.

That which I am since I was born, that will die and fall to nothing, for it is mortal; and so it must, in time, decay.

If you do not understand these words, do not trouble your heart with them. It is an undisguised truth, coming directly from the Heart of God.

Gott als Vater, Gott als Mutter[3]

Gott ist nicht allein ein Vater aller Dinge,
er ist vielmehr auch eine Mutter aller Dinge.

Denn er ist darum ein Vater, weil er eine Ursache und ein Schöpfer aller Dinge ist.

Er ist aber auch eine Mutter aller Dinge, denn wenn die Kreatur von ihm ihr Wesen nimmt, so bleibt er bei der Kreatur und erhält sie in ihrem Wesen.

●

Einige Leute glauben, sie sollten Gott sehen, als stünder er da und sie hier. Dem ist nicht so. Gott und ich, wir sind eins.

Durch das Erkennen, nehme ich Gott in mich hinein. Durch die Liebe hingegen, gehe ich in Gott ein.

---

[3] In seiner Arbeit als wandernder Prediger, Lehrer und Berater besuchte Eckhart auch die Frauenklöster, z.B. der Beginen, die von der kirchlichen Hierarchie vernachlässigt oder gar unterdrückt wurden. Seine mystische Vision hatte ihn zu der Erkenntis gebracht, dass die Gottheit Männliche und Weibliche Aspekte einschliesst.

God the Father, God the Mother[4]

God is not only the Father of all things,
but also the Mother of all things.

God is the Father, because he is the originator and creator of all things.

God is also the Mother, who sustains and maintains all created beings, as they
derive their essence beingness from God.

●

Some people think they should be able to see God standing there, while they
are here. This is not how it is. God and I are at one.

Through knowledge, I take God into myself. Through love, I enter into God.

---

[4] In his work as an itinerant preacher, Eckhart included in his journeys of teaching and counseling commu-
nities of nuns, like the Begines, who were often neglected or even oppressed by the ecclesiastical hierarchy.
His mystical vision had taken him to a recognition of Deity that included both male and female principles.

Johann Wolfgang von Goethe
Gingko Biloba[1]

Dieses Baum's Blatt, der von Osten
Meinem Garten anvertraut,
Gibt geheimen Sinn zu kosten,
Wie's den Wissenden erbaut.

Ist es ein lebendig Wesen,
Das sich in sich selbst getrennt?
Sind es zwei, die sich erlesen,
Dass man sie als eines kennt?

Solche Fragen zu erwidern,
Fand ich wohl den rechten Sinn;
Fühlst Du nicht an meinen Liedern,
Dass ich eins und doppelt bin?

---

[1] Goethe (1749-1832) hat als Erster den Gingko Baum in Europa aus Asien eingeführt und in seinem Garten gepflanzt. *Gingko biloba* ist einer der ältesten Pflanzen im evolutionären Sinn. Ein Gingkobaum ist als einziges Lebewesen am Nullpunkt der atomaren Explosion in Hiroshima stehen geblieben. In heutiger Zeit hat man entdeckt, dass ein Extrakt des Gingkoblattes die Gehirndurchblutung fördert und daher das Gedächtnis stärkt. Ob Goethes Zeilen über "geheimen Sinn" und "den Wissenden erbaut" darauf hindeuten, wissen wir nicht.

Johann Wolfgang von Goethe
Gingko Biloba[2]

The leaf of this tree from the East
which in my garden has come to grow,
makes of secret meaning a feast,
so delightful for those who know.

Is this leaf one living being,
that has divided itself in twain?
Or is it a pair we are seeing,
becoming a oneness again?

To answer this question well,
I pondered and thought it through:
From my poems and songs can't you tell
that my being is one – and yet two?

---

[2] Goethe (1749-1832), who was a botanist and geologist in addition to being poet, dramatist and novelist, introduced the Gingko tree into Europe from its native Asia, and planted one in his garden. *Gingko biloba* is one of the world's oldest plants, in an evolutionary sense. It is also one of the hardiest, being the only living being left standing at ground zero after the atomic explosion in Hiroshima. In modern times, extracts of Gingko have been shown to increase blood circulation in the brain, and hence improve memory. Whether Goethe's lines about "secret meaning" and "those who know" point to that effect, is not known.

Eins und Alles

Im Grenzenlosen sich zu finden,
Wird gern der Einzelne verschwinden,
Da löst sich aller Überdruss.
Statt heissen Wünschen, wilden Wollen,
Statt läst'gem Fordern, strengen Sollen,
Sich aufzugeben ist Genuss.

Weltseele, komm, mich zu durchdringen!
Dann mit dem Weltgeist selbst zu ringen
Wird unserer Kräfte Hochberuf.
Teilnehmend führen gute Geister,
Gelinde leitend, höchste Meister,
Zu dem, der alles schafft und schuf.

Und umzuschaffen das Geschaffne,
Damit sich's nicht zum Starren waffne,
Wirkt ewiges lebendiges Tun.
Und was nicht war, nun will es werden,
Zu reinen Sonnen, farbigen Erden,
In keinem Falle darf es ruhn.

Es soll sich regen, schaffend handeln,
Erst sich gestalten, dann werwandeln;
Nur scheinbar steht's Momente still.
Das Ewige regt sich fort in allen:
Denn alles muss in Nichts zerfallen,
Wenn es im Sein beharren will.

One and Everything

To find yourself in boundlessness
and vanish as a separate self,
brings dissolution of distress.
No more wishing, nor wild wanting,
no vexing claims, nor strict demands,
Instead – a joyous giving up of self.

Soul of the world, come permeate my being!
In wrestling with the spirit of the world,
we find our nature's highest calling.
We're led by spirits, with compassion,
by highest masters, gently guided,
to the One creating everything.

To recreate what's been created,
prevents defensive hardening –
this ceaseless doing of our lives.
For what was not, now will it be –
these radiant suns and brilliant earths,
always changing, never resting.

There's movement and creative doing,
self first forming, then transforming,
it only seems, at time, to stop.
The Eternal moves in everything:
for everything must fall to nothing,
in order to remain in being.

Zwei Seelen wohnen, ach, in meiner Brust[3]

Zwei Seelen wohnen, ach, in meiner Brust,
Die eine will sich von der anderen trennen:
Die eine hält, in derber Liebeslust,
Sich an die Welt mit klammernden Organen;
Die andere hebt gewaltsam sich vom Dunst
Zu den Gefilden hoher Ahnen.

O gibt es Geister in der Luft,
Die zwischen Erd und Himmel herrschend weben,
So steiget nieder aus dem goldnen Duft
Und führt mich weg zu neuem, bunten Leben!

---

[3] Aus *Faust I*. In meinem Buch *Das Mystische Grün*, schrieb ich "der oppositionelle Dualismus zwischen Geist und Natur entwickelte sich aus dem jüdisch-christlichen Monotheismus. ...Bis weit in die Moderne scheint diese Trennung in wichtigen und einflussreichen Schriften auf. Eine der eindrucksvollsten Formulierungen finden wir in Goethe's *Faust*. Das Drama von Faust, der ruheloss und rücksichtslos nach Wissen als persönliche Macht strebt, scheint ein Schlüssel zur Europäischen Psyche zu sein. Man kann sagen dass es durch die gesamte Entwicklung der westlichen Kultur hindurch es diese Vorstellung von zwei Selbst-Seelen gegeben hat – ein natürliches Selbst, irdisch und organisch, mit nach unten gerichteter Tendenz, und ein anderes Selbst, geistig und ätherisch, mit nach oben gerichteter Tendenz."

Two souls, alas, are living in my breast[4]

Two souls, alas, are living in my breast,
Each striving to be separate from the other:
One of them clings tightly to the world,
With passionate desire for sensations;
The other lifts forcefully from earth's haze,
To the realms of high ancestral spirits.

If there be ruling spirits of the air
That float between the earth and sky,
Descend, I beg you, from the golden realms,
And sweep me forth to rainbow-colored life!

---

[4] From *Faust I*. In my book *Green Psychology*, I wrote, "the oppositional dualism between spirit and nature grew out of Judeo-Christian transcendental monotheism. Even well into the modern age, we find this same separation appearing in influential writings. ...The 18th century German poet-philosopher Goethe formulated this core dualistic image in a famous passage in his drama *Faust*. The story of Faust, with his restless and ruthless quest for knowledge as personal power, strikes us as somehow a mythic key to the European psyche. We could say that throughout the history of Western culture there has been a conception of two self-souls – a natural self, which is earthy-organic and tends downward, and a spiritual or mental self, which is airy-ethereal and tends upward."

William Blake[1]
Die Hochzeit des Himmels und der Hölle – I

Die alten Dichter haben alle wahrnehmbare Objekte mit Göttern oder
Genien belebt, sie mit Namen benannt, und sie geschmückt mit den
Eigenschaften der Wälder, Flüsse, Berge, Seen, Städte, und was alles ihre
erweiterten und vielfältigen Sinne wahrnehmen konnten.
Und insbesondere studierten sie den Genius jeder Stadt und jedes
Landes, und stellten diese unter ihre geistige Gottheit.

Bis ein System geschaffen wurde, das gewisse Leute ausnutzten, um das
gemeine Volk zu versklaven, indem sie versuchten, die geistigen
Gottheiten von ihren Objekten abzutrennen und zu abstrahieren –
Und so entstand das Priestertum. Die Formen des Gottesdienstes
wurden aus dichterischen Erzählungen genommen.
Dann verkündigten sie, dass die Götter es so angeordnet hätten.

So haben die Menschen vergessen, dass alle Gottheiten in der
menschlichen Brust innewohnen.

---

[1] William Blake (1757-1827)

William Blake²

The Marriage of Heaven and Hell – I

The ancient poets animated all sensible objects with gods or geniuses, calling them by the names and adorning them with the properties of woods, rivers, mountains, lakes, cities, nations, and whatever their enlarged and numerous senses could perceive.
And particularly they studied the genius of each city and country, placing it under its mental deity.

Till a system was formed, which some took advantage of and enslaved the vulgar by attempting to realize or abstract the mental deities from their objects: thus began priesthood.
Choosing forms of worship from poetic tales.
And at length they pronounced that the gods had ordered such things.

Thus men forgot that all deities reside in the human breast.

---

² William Blake (1757-1827)

Die Hochzeit des Himmels und der Hölle – II

Die uralte Tradition, dass die Welt durch Feuer zerstört wird
am Ende von sechs tausend Jahren ist wahr, so wie ich es von der
Hölle gehört habe.

Denn dem Cherub mit seinem flammenden Schwert wird dann
befohlen, seine Wacht am Baum des Lebens zu verlassen, und wenn
er das tut, wird die ganze Schöpfung versehrt und erscheint dann
unendlich und heilig, während sie jetzt endlich und verdorben erscheint.

Das alles wird zu Stande kommen durch eine Verfeinerung der
sinnlichen Freude.

Aber zuerst muss die Idee, dass der Mensch einen Körper
getrennt von seiner Seele hat, ausgemerzt werden: dies werde ich tun
durch das Drucken mit der höllischen Method der Ätzung. In der Hölle
wirken die Ätzmittel heilend und medizinisch, weil sie die Oberflächen
abschmelzen, und das Unendliche, das verborgen war, offenbaren.

Wenn die Tore der Wahrnehmung gereinigt werden, dann
erscheint jegliches Ding so wie es ist: unendlich.

Denn der Mensch hat sich eingeschlossen und sieht alles nur
durch die engen Spalten seiner Höhle.

The Marriage of Heaven and Hell – II

The ancient tradition that the world will be consumed in fire at the end of six thousand years is true, as I have heard from Hell.

For the cherub with his flaming sword is thereby commanded to leave his guard at the tree of life, and when he does, the whole creation will be consumed, and appear infinite and holy, whereas it now appears finite and corrupt.

This will come to pass by an improvement of sensual enjoyment.

But first the notion that man has a body distinct from his soul, is to be expunged: this I shall do by printing in the infernal method, by corrosives, which in Hell are salutary and medicinal, melting apparent surfaces away and displaying the Infinite which was hid.

If the doors of perception were cleansed, everything would appear to man as it is: infinite.

For man has closed himself up, till he sees all things through narrow chinks of his cavern.

Giftiger Baum[3]

Zum Freund war mein Gemüt
so schwer wie Blei.
Ich sagt' es ihm ganz schlicht –
Dann war ich frei.

Zum Feind war auch mein Herz
Mit Groll so schwer.
Ich sagt' ihm nichts,
Mein Groll wuchs mehr.

Hab' ihn bewässert mit meinen Tränen,
Und meinen Ängsten, Tag und Nacht.
Hab' ihn bestrahlt mit sonnigem Lächeln,
Mit sanfter, falscher List bedacht.

Der Baum des Grolls wuchs Tag und Nacht,
Ein schöner Apfel hing im Glanz.
Mein Feind, der sah die schöne Frucht,
Und sah auch: sie gehört mir ganz.

Als die Nacht die Welt verdunkelt,
Mein Feind in meinen Garten schlich.
Den Feind am Boden tod zu sehen,
Am nächsten Morgen, freut' es mich.

---

[3] Blakes erste Strophe habe ich als zwei Strophen übersetzt.

A Poison Tree[4]

I was angry with my friend:
I told my wrath, my wrath did end.
I was angry with my foe:
I told it not, my wrath did grow.

And I water'd it in fears,
Night & morning with my tears;
And I sunned it with smiles,
And with soft deceitful wiles.

And it grew both day and night,
Till it bore an apple bright;
And my foe beheld it shine,
And he knew that it was mine,

And into my garden stole
When the night had veil'd the pole:
In the morning glad I see
My foe outstretch'd beneath the tree.

---

[4] In my German version the first verse is translated as two verses.

Anzeichen der Unschuld

Gewoben haben Lust und Leid
Der Menschenseele feines Kleid.
Hinter jedem Gram und Pein
Zieht die Freude Faden fein.

●

Will man die Freude an sich binden,
Wird ihr beflügeltes Leben verschwinden.
Aber wer die Freude küsst im fliegen
Kann in der Sonne der Ewigkeit liegen.

●

Eine Welt zu seh'n im Körnchen Sand
Den Himmel im wilden Blumengrunde,
Unendlichkeit halten in der Hand
Und Ewigkeit in einer Stunde.

Auguries of Innocence

Joy and Woe are woven fine
A clothing for the soul divine.
Under every grief and pine
Runs a joy with silken twine.

●

He who binds to himself a joy,
Doth its wingéd life destroy.
But he who kisses the joy as it flies,
Lives in Eternity's sunrise

●

To see a world in a Grain of Sand
And Heaven in a Wild Flower,
Hold Infinity in the palm of your hand
And eternity in an hour.

Rainer Maria Rilke[1]

Imaginärer Lebenslauf

Ernst eine Kindheit, grenzenlos und ohne
Verzicht und Ziel. O unbewusste Lust.
Auf einmal Schrecken, Schranke, Schule, Frohne
Und Absturz in Versuchung und Verlust.

Trotz. Der Gebogene wird selber Bieger
und rächt an anderen, dass er erlag.
Geliebt, gefürchtet, Retter, Ringer, Sieger
Und Überwinder, Schlag auf Schlag.

Und dann allein im Weiten, Leichten, Kalten.
Doch tief in der errichteten Gestalt
ein Atemholen nach dem Ersten, Alten…

Da stürzte Gott aus seinem Hinterhalt.

---

[1] Rainer Maria Rilke (1875-1926)

Rainer Maria Rilke[2]

Imaginary Life Story

First - a childhood, without limits,
no denials and no goals. Such innocent joy!
Then suddenly - alarm, boundaries, schoolrooms, cages,
plunging into temptation and deep loss.

Defiance. One who was beaten, becomes a beater now,
taking revenge for his own defeats.
Loved and feared, the rescuer, fighter, winner,
he overpowers others, blow by blow.

And then…alone, in vastness, lightness, cold.
From deep within the upright human form,
He draws a breath, from the ancient source.

Then all at once, God burst out of hiding.

---

[2] Rainer Maria Rilke (1875-1926)

Das Letzte Haus[3]

In diesem Dorfe steht das letzte Haus
so einsam wie das letzte Haus der Welt.

Die Strasse, die das kleine Dorf nicht hält,
geht langsam weiter in die Nacht hinaus.

Das kleine Dorf ist nur ein Übergang
zwischen zwei Weiten, ahnungsvoll und bang,
ein Weg an Häusern hin statt eines Stegs.

Und die das Dorf verlassen, wandern lang,
und viele sterben vielleicht unterwegs.

---

[3] *Das Stundenbuch, Buch II: Von der Pilgerschaft. 1901.*

The Last House[4]

In this village the last house stands alone,
as though it were the last house in the world.

The road, which the small village can't contain,
slowly goes far beyond into the night.

The small village is only a crossing place,
between two vast spaces, foreboding and anxious,
a path along houses, not a footbridge.

And those who leave the village, wander far,
and many perhaps die along the way.

---

[4] *The Book of Hours II: Pilgrimage. 1901.*

Bertholt Brecht[1]

An die Nachgeborenen

Wirklich, ich lebe in finsteren Zeiten!
Das arglose Wort ist töricht. Eine glatte Stirn
Deutet auf Unempfindlichkeit hin. Der Lachende
Hat die furchtbare Nachricht
Nur noch nicht empfangen.

Was sind das für Zeiten, wo
Ein Gespräch über Bäume fast ein Verbrechen ist
Weil es ein Schweigen über so viele Untaten einschliesst!
Der dort ruhig über die Strasse geht
Ist wohl nicht mehr erreichbar für seine Freunde
Die in Not sind?

Es ist wahr: ich verdiene noch meinen Unterhalt
Aber glaubt mir: das ist nur ein Zufall. Nichts
Von dem, was ich tue, berechtigt mich dazu, mich satt zuessen.
Zufällig bin ich verschont. (Wenn mein Glück aussetzt, bin ich verloren.)

Man sagt mir: Iss und trink du! Sei froh, dass du hast!
Aber wie kann ich essen und trinken, wenn
ich dem Hungernden entreisse, was ich esse, und
Mein Glas Wasser einem Verdurstenden fehlt?
Und doch esse und trinke ich.

Ich wäre gerne auch weise.
In den alten Büchern steht, was weise ist:
Sich aus dem Streit der Welt halten und die kurze Zeit
Ohne Furcht verbringen
Auch ohne Gewalt auskommen
Böses mit Gutem vergelten
Seine Wünsche nicht erfüllen, sondern vergessen
Gilt für Weise.
Alles das kann ich nicht:
Wirklich, ich lebe in finsteren Zeiten!

---

[1] *Bertholt Brecht* (1898-1956). Ich schätze dieses Gedicht, weil es das Leben in Zeiten des Krieges und des Faschismus stoisch, doch mit Empathie betrachtet.

Bertholt Brecht

To Those Born After Us[2]

Truly, I live in a time of darkness!
The innocent word is foolish. A smooth brow
Suggests lack of sensitivity. Those who are laughing
Just haven't heard
The terrible news yet.

What kind of times are these,
When a conversation about trees is almost a crime,
Because so many misdeeds are left unspoken?
That person there – calmly crossing the street,
Is probably no longer available
To his friends who are in trouble.

It's true: I'm still earning a living.
But that's pure coincidence.
Nothing in what I do justifies my eating my fill.
By chance, I am spared. (When my luck runs out, I'm lost).

People say to me: Eat and drink! Be glad that you can.
But how can I eat and drink, when what I eat
Is taken from the mouths of the hungry, and the
Water I drink deprives one who is thirsty?
But still…I eat and I drink.

I would like to be wise.
In ancient books one can read what is wise:
To not participate in the conflicts of the world,
To be without fear, in the short time we have,
Also to get along without violence,
To requite evil with good
To not satisfy one's desires, but to forget them –
These things are considered wise.
All of them are beyond me.
Truly I live in a time of darkness!

---

[2] *Bertholt Brecht* (1898-1956). I treasure this poem because of the way it regards life in a time of war and fascism stoically, but with empathy.

In die Städte kam ich zur Zeit der Unordnung
Als da Hunger herrschte.
Unter die Menschen kam ich zu der Zeit des Aufruhrs
Und ich empörte mich mit ihnen.
So verging meine Zeit
Die auf Erden mir gegeben war.

Mein Essen ass ich zwischen den Schlachten
Schlafen legte ich mich unter die Mörder.
Der Liebe pflegte ich achtlos
Und die Natur sah ich ohne Geduld.
So verging meine Zeit
Die auf Erden mir gegeben war.

Die Strassen führten in dem Sumpf zu meiner Zeit.
Die Sprache verriet mich dem Schlächter.
Ich vermochte nur wenig. Aber die Herrschenden
Sassen ohne mich sicherer, das hoffte ich.
So verging meine Zeit
Die auf Erden mir gegeben war.

Die Kräfte waren gering. Das Ziel
Lag in grosser Ferne.
Es war deutlich sichtbar, wenn auch für mich
Kaum zu erreichen.
So verging meine Zeit
Die auf Erden mir gegeben war.

I came into the cities at a time of disorder,
A time of hunger.
I came among people at a time of uproar,
And I was outraged with them.
So passed the time
I was given on Earth.

I took food between battles
And laid down to sleep among killers.
I was careless in love,
And regarded nature without patience.
So passed the time
I was given on Earth.

In my time, all roads led to a swamp.
My language gave me away to the executioner.
I could do very little. But the rulers
Sat more securely without me – that was my hope.
So passed the time
I was given on Earth.

Our means were meager. The goal
Was far away.
It was clearly visible, even though,
For me, it was not attainable.
So passed the time
I was given on Earth.

Ihr, die ihr auftauchen werdet aus der Flut
In der wir untergegangen sind
Gedenkt
Wenn Ihr von unseren Schwächen sprecht
Auch der finsteren Zeit
Der ihr entronnen seid.

Gingen wir doch, öfter als die Schuhe die Länder wechselnd.
Durch die Kriege der Klassen, verzweifelt
Wenn da nur Unrecht war und keine Empörung.

Dabei wissen wir doch:
Auch der Hass gegen die Niedrigkeit
Verzerrt die Züge.
Auch der Zorn über das Unrecht
Macht die Stimme heiser. Ach, wir
Die wir den Boden bereiten wollten für Freundlichkeit
Konnten selbst nicht freundlich sein.

Ihr aber, wenn es so weit sein wird
Dass der Mensch dem Menschen ein Helfer ist
Gedenkt unsrer
Mit Nachsicht.

You, who are the ones who will rise up
From the flood in which we went down,
Remember
When you speak of our weaknesses,
The dark times
from which you escaped.

We travelled, changing countries more often than shoes,
Through the wars between classes, in despair
Because we found injustice, but no outrage.

And yet we do know this:
Hatred, even of meanness,
Distorts the visage.
Anger, even at injustice,
Makes hoarse the voice. Alas,
Though we wanted to prepare the ground for kindness,
We didn't know how to be kind ourselves.

But you, when the time comes,
When human beings can help one another,
Remember us
With forbearance.

EPILOG I
Heraclitus
ethos anthropoi daimon[1]

Oft übersetzt:
Der Charakter eines Menschen bestimmt sein Schicksal.

ethos   Sitte, Brauch, Werte, Gewohnheit, Charakter; vergleichbar mit Lateinisch *mores*.
anthropoi des Menschen.
daimon   Göttlicher Geist; auch – Schicksal, Geschick.

Also, mit Berücksichtigung der unten angegebenen, ursprünglischen Bedeutung von *daimon,* wäre eine alternative Übersetzung:

Der Charakter des Menschen wird bestimmt oder geleitet von seinem göttlichen Geist.

---

[1] *Daimon(es)* – In der alten griechischen Religion und Mythologie sind *daimones* übernatürliche Wesen zwischen Göttern und Menschen. Bei Homer sind die Worte *daimones* und *theoi* (Götter) fast gleichbedeutend, doch spätere Autoren wie Platon entwickelten einen Unterschied zwischen ihnen. In Platon's *Symposium* belehrt die Priesterin Diotima den Sokrates, dass die *Liebe* kein Gott ist sondern ein "grosser *Daimon*." Sie erklärt weiter, dass "alles Daimonische zwischen dem Göttlichem und dem Sterblichem ist" und dass die *Daimones* Menschliches zu den Göttern bringen, und göttliche Anweisungen zu den Menschen."

    Daimones wurden nicht als böse Geister angesehen; eher sind sie Schutzgeister. Vergleichbar ist der römische *Genius* – der einen Menschen begleitet und inspiriert; oder als *Genius loci* einen Ort beschützt.

    Hellenistische Autoren unterschieden zwischen *Eudaimones* (guten Geistern) und *Kakodaimones* (bösen Geistern). Die *Eudaimones* waren Schutzengeln ähnlich. Die *Kakodaimones* wurden in die Dämonen der Christlichen Kirchenväter verwandelt – böse Geister die die Menschen mit üblen Gedanken und Impulsen belästigen, versuchen und besetzen.

EPILOG I

Heraclitus

ethos anthropoi daimon[2]

Often translated:
A man's character determines his fate or destiny.

ethos   character, ethics, values, ethos; compare Latin – *mores*.
anthropoi   of man;
daimon   Divine Spirit; also – destiny.

So, in consideration of the orginal, spiritual meaning of *daimon* (see below) an alternative translation would be:

A man's character is determined by, or guided by, his Divine Spirit.

---

[2]   *Daimon(es)* – in ancient Greek religion and mythology, *daimones* are supernatural beings between humans and gods. In Homer the words *theoi* (gods) and *daimones* were practically synonymous, but later writers like Plato developed a distinction between the two. In Plato's *Symposium* the priestess Diotima teaches Socrates that *love* is not a god, but rather a "great daimon." She explains that "everything daimonic is between divine and mortal" and she says *daimones* "interpret and transport human things to the gods and divine things to men."

     Daimones were not considered evil; they were more like protective deities or spirits. A comparable Roman/Latin *genius* accompanied and inspired a person; or as *genius loci*, protected a place.

     Hellenistic writers distinguished *eudaimones* (good spirits) and *kakodaimones* (evil spirits). The *eudaimones* were equivalent to guardian angels or guiding spirits. The *kakodaimones* were transformed into the *demons* of the Christian patristic writers – malignant spirits that harrassed, tempted and possessed humans with evil thoughts and impulses.

EPILOG II

Talmud oder Unbekannter Autor

Achte auf Deine Gedanken[1]

Achte auf deine Gedanken,
  denn sie werden Worte.

Achte auf deine Worte,
  denn sie werden Taten.

Achte auf deine Taten,
  denn sie werden Gewohnheiten.

Achte auf deine Gewohnheiten,
  denn sie werden dein Charakter.

Achte auf deinen Charakter,
  denn das wird dein Schicksal.[2]

---

[1] Diese Zeilen, oder Variationen davon, sind einer Vielfalt von Quellen zugeschrieben worden, obwohl keine eindeutig bewiesen ist. Bei einer Google Suche, findet man sie dem *Talmud* zugeschrieben; auch zu frühen Schriften der Christlichen Kirchenväter; zu Hazrat Ali Haider, dem Vierten Gerechten Kalif; zu jemandem mit Namen "Frank Outlaw," über den nichts Weiteres bekannt ist; zu Ralph Waldo Emerson; zu dem Thai Buddhistischem Mönch des 20. Jahrhundert, Achann Chaa von Wat Po Pongto; zu einer Frau namens "Elizabeth C." die behauptet, sie hätte diese Zeilen1998 geschrieben…und möglicherweise zu anderen.

[2] Der Satz "Dein Charakter bestimmt dein Schicksal" entspricht genau einem berühmten Satz des Heraklit, dem Griechischem Philosophen des 6. Jahrhundert v. Chr. – *ethos anthropoi daimon*. Dieser Satz wird meistens übersetzt als "Des Menschen Charakter bestimmt sein Schicksal." (s. Epilog I)

EPILOG II

Talmud *or* **Unknown Author**

Take Care of Your Thoughts[3]

Take care of your thoughts,
   for they will become words.

Take care of your words,
   for they will become actions.

Take care of your actions,
   for they will become habits.

Take care of your habits,
   for they will become your character.

Take care of your character,
   for that will shape your destiny.[4]

---

[3] These lines, or variations of them, have been attributed to a wide variety of authors, though none of them are conclusively documented. A Google search found them credited to the *Talmud*; to early Christian patristic writers, who relate it to the value of "watchfulness;" to Hazrat Ali Haider, the Fourth Righteous Caliph; to someone called "Frank Outlaw," about whom nothing else is known; to Ralph Waldo Emerson; to the 20th century Thai Buddhist monk Achann Chaa of Wat Po Pongto; to a woman named "Elizabeth C." who claimed to have written them in 1998…and perhaps to others.

[4] The statement "your character will form your destiny" corresponds exactly to one of the most famous epigrams of Heraclitus, the 6th century BC Greek philosopher: *ethos anthropoi daimon*. This epigram is usually translated as "A man's character determines his fate." (see Epilog I)

www.ingramcontent.com/pod-product-compliance
Lightning Source LLC
Chambersburg PA
CBHW020920140626
46545CB00015B/1025